Genevieve Snell

Rhymes like These

Illustrations by Liz Stutz

Pegasus

NIGHTINGALE PAPERBACK

A CIP catalogue record for this title is
available from the British Library.

ISBN 978-1-80468-057-5

Nightingale Books is an imprint of
Pegasus Elliot MacKenzie Publishers Ltd.
www.pegasuspublishers.com

First Published in 2024

Nightingale Books
Sheraton House Castle Park
Cambridge England

Printed & Bound in Great Britain

Dedication

This one is for my wonderful mum and dad...
there are no words for how much I love and
miss you both. Thank you for the abundance
of love and laughter. But mostly thank you
for those last words when you whispered
that I am your favourite daughter. I won't
tell Joss.

The Hare and the Tortoise (Claire and Hortense)

Claire and Hortense were 'friends from work'
Hortense was a grafter, Claire would shirk...
If they met any other way, they'd not give each other
the time of day.

Yet Claire and Hortense thought alike on one issue
Their desire to be rid of their own 'fatty tissue'
(Neither one was actually fat, but have you ever tried
telling a woman that?)

But it can be agreed, both had wobbly bits
Claire had the thighs, Hortense had the tits
Show me a woman who's perfect – bottom to top –
and I will show you: photoshop.

They both decided it was dieting time
But each had a different diet in mind.

Claire's approach was to 'get thin quick'
She was willing to try any weight-loss trick.

She decided first on a fitness regime
True to type, it was somewhat extreme
Up at six for a run, swim and weights,
cardio at lunch and Pilates at eight
She stuck to this plan for a day and a half
Then said, "Exercise? You're 'avin a laugh."

Hortense's approach was calmer than Claire's
She cut out all chocolate and took the stairs.

Claire's next move was a detox drink
After a sip, it was poured down the sink
"This green drink is grim, it's utterly vile...
My next move shall be: extreme self-denial."

For (almost) a full morning, she ate nothing at all
It was hard, she was practically climbing the wall
Then Sue from accounts brought birthday cake in,
and 'extreme self-denial' went straight in the bin.

Hortense, meanwhile, decreased portion size
And made the heartbreaking decision to stop eating pies.

Claire changed course to the 'super food' route
"I will survive on seeds, salad and fruit."
She stocked up on kale and made things from spelt
But the more she ate, the worse she felt
Perhaps, she thought, I'm not made for buckwheat
I shall leave such foods to the dieting elite...

Hortense upped her game and ran 2K
While counting her calorie intake each day.

In desperation, Claire searched online
"These fat fighting diet pills have to be mine."
To pay for the pills, she remortgaged her flat
"Surely, it's worth it to get rid of this fat?"
Sadly, the side effects listed were scary –
"To get rid of the fat I might end up hairy?"

During this time Hort's fitness improved
And her weight decreased, the more she moved.

But Claire had actually put on an amount
"Damn it," she hissed, "I blame Sue from accounts."

So, even with diets, we should surely embrace
That slow and steady does indeed win the race.

Maybe Baby

Sooo... this topic is undoubtedly the most complex of themes
And it actually begins way back in our teens.

Those days the word 'pregnant' struck fear in our hearts
And we believed it could happen if we bumped body parts.

For the next ten (or so) years, we used condoms or pills
To prevent making babies from rogue penis-spills.

Then, overnight, we make a decision:
We've met the right man, we want a family addition
Or it may be a woman, or the timing that's right;
whatever the case, we've a baby in sight.

This is when we discover it's not as easy as we thought
And our sex life immediately becomes
stressful and fraught.

For some, of course, it happens in days
After less than a handful of bedroom forays
In such cases, the man will reflect rather sadly,
that the fun was short lived –
she'd never bonked him so gladly!

But for most of us, it comes as quite a surprise
That making a baby takes quite a few tries.

It involves thermometers, positions and
consulting physicians
In desperation, some even try superstitions
(I, myself, have climbed through a hole, believing the
myth of the Cornish 'Mên-an-Tol'.) 1 Google it.

If we're incredibly lucky, there is finally the time
When that Clearblue test clearly shows us two lines
(Our relationship with test strips is really quite strange
– when reading results, we can look quite deranged.
We twist it, we turn it, we hold it up to the light,
until at last the result is what we think is right.)

So we've been granted our wish –
we are growing a person
Who knew that the worrying would actually
now worsen?

A common panic occurs when with guilt we remember
That two weeks ago, we went on that bender.

Straight on to Google – we search 'baby' and 'booze'
Until a link says it's fine – and that's the link that
we choose
But as soon as that worry has been put to bed,
an army of others lay siege to our head.

Will my baby be healthy? Will I be a good mum?
Is this now the permanent size of my bum?
And this is before a bump's even in view – since
Clearblue said yes, you've been eating for two.

You live the next three months on the edge of a knife
Quite frankly, the longest twelve weeks of your life.

And when at last you can share the news
that you're blessed
You find that most people had already guessed
To be honest, they found it quite idiotic,
that you blamed 'not drinking' on antibiotics...
(The girls at work had also guessed,
due to the upgraded size of your breasts.)

For the next three months, life is quite cheerful
You are proud of your bump, you are not yet too fearful.

You read every book, you research 'natural birth'
You consider yourself to be 'Mother Earth'.

In your third trimester – yes, that's a word you now use
(as are perineum, colostrum, Lamaze and ventouse)
You are told that while birthing, some women do poos...
You are filled with horror as you have yet to grasp that at
that point, you won't care what comes out of your arse.

It is finally time to join antenatal classes
Where you learn about 'Birth Plans'
and other such farces
(When you squeeze a small person from your front
bottom, you may find that your 'Birth Plan'
is mostly forgotten...)

And then, finally, it's here... your baby's 'due date'
And you realise you are in for another darned wait...
2Please see 'Definitely Baby' for further details

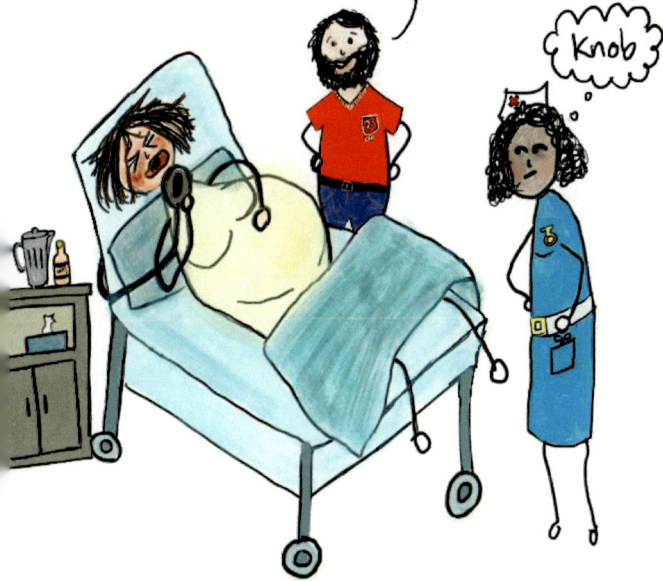

Definitely Baby

Your due date is here... but your baby is not
Quite frankly, you may actually soon lose the plot.

You've walked, you've massaged, you've even tried sex
You've poured gallons of raspberry tea down your neck.

And then finally – after all that waiting and waiting
You realise your waters are actually breaking
At first, you thought you'd embarrassed yourself and it
was time to head to the TENA shelf.

But the cramps begin and it's then that it clicks:
This time it is not Braxton-fucking-Hicks.

So you dial your partner (or your birth buddy of choice)
And try to keep the panic out of your voice
Of course, they don't answer when you call the first time
– in the months to come, they will pay for this crime.

When, at last, they finally appear
You are pretty darned sure that delivery is near.

So you arrive at the hospital, on that day long awaited
And they tell you, you are only 2 cm dilated...
You are sent back home, advised to eat curry
And told not to come back in any great hurry.

Back at home, you pace, you drink more effing tea
Frantically hoping to dilate a degree...
In desperation, you even resort to more sex
The position required is somewhat complex.

Your partner channel-hops to 'keep up your spirits'
This fails when they linger on 'One Born Every Minute'.

You wait six more hours (it seems like eternity)
Before heading back to the ward of maternity.

One further inelegant 'exam' later
You are deemed to be an appropriate dilator
(Who knew it would ever be such a thing, to be judged
on the size of your 'down there' ring?)

It's at this point you realise you need every drug going
If you're expected to keep this birth malarkey flowing

And that's when they decide to make the decree
"You are too far along, dear... You've to do it drug free."

You scream, you shout, you HATE the kid's dad
The swear words you use are the ones that are BAD
(The hospital actually took quite an affront...
Apparently, you can't call a nurse a c***.)

The room's full of people saying 'breathe' or 'push'
They mostly direct these words at your bush
And, needless to say, you've not recently waxed,
hair is protruding from all of your cracks.

Can I take this moment to apologise for my wording?
It seems to have morphed into a language disturbing...
The guttersnipe way I used my own birthing voice may
of course not reflect everyone's choice.

You continue to push (and, in my case, to swear)
As everyone tells you, you're nearly there.

They say 'one last push' and you're sure they are lying
Until you hear that beautiful crying.

And finally... FINALLY... your baby is here
And why you went through this is utterly clear.

For of all the women to ever give birth
You've borne the most perfect child on this earth.

"So yeah... And I didn't even know that could happen... But they poked it all back in and stitched me up like a bit of brisket, then sent me home with paracetamol and a pamphlet on clenching. Oh, I'm Nicky by the way."

Left Holding the Baby

So here you are... the greatest woman on Earth
Pretty much the ONLY WOMAN WHO EVER GAVE BIRTH
(Okay, you know that's not strictly true, but you're
pretty darned pleased with your birthing debut.)

You've shown the nurses you can change a nappy
You've managed one feed (which makes the midwife SO happy)
By 'feed', I mean your baby's glanced at your boob –
you've no idea if it knows it's for food.

You see, it turns out breastfeeding's not as easy as it looks
Not the 'effortless act of nature' that's portrayed in the books
We all know that breast milk's a baby's choice tipple...
but this does require an obliging nipple...

Nevertheless, you're deemed ready for release
You're quite pleased to escape the breast-feeding police...

Back at home, you feel truly amazing
Lying back, babe in arms, enjoying the praising.

Actually, no – it doesn't quite work like that
For one thing, it seems you're still rather fat
Plus your front bottom stings, your boobs are like rocks
and you find you're still wearing maternity frocks.

Despite the above, the first week is okay
As a stream of well-wishers fill your day.

Everyone agrees you've made the most perfect baby
You revel in being such a brave, clever lady
Also, your partner is still off work, which means
there are loads of jobs you can shirk.

I can't fold shirts – my front bottom still hurts
I can't lift a mop – my C-section might pop
I can't cut the grass – I've stitches in my arse
Whatever the damage to your undercarriage,
the burden of pain can be turned to your gain.

However, week two brings a few warning signs
That everything might in fact not be so fine.

You cry inexplicably, your nipples red raw
You're still rather fat, your front bottom still sore.

The health visitor's checklist indicates you're depressed
You shout, "So would you be, if these were your breasts."

Your partner has naffed back off to the office
His attempt to look sad brings you no solace.
(To be honest, you suspect he's rather relieved –
a less charitable word might even be pleased)

So, out comes the pram out for the 'baby group' circuit
That is, of course, if you could only work it
The car seat was tricky, but this pram contraption?!
They lied when they sold it as 'easy retraction'.

You finally leave the house on attempt number four
You've dealt with pee, poo and vomit before you reach
the front door.

So... the 'baby group' thang... oh, where to begin
But, please, fear not – you will absolutely fit in.

Every group has its 'mum types' – it's rather uncanny
'Gina Ford', 'Demand Feeding' or 'I've got a nanny'.

There's also a divide between 'I'm Mother Earth'
Or the other extreme – 'Get me the hell back to work'.

These differences aside – it is here you will find
A BFF (or two) who brings you some peace of mind.

For there is nothing that bonds a group of fat ladies
Like discussing the sleep and poo of their babies.

Forty Something

Remember when we were back in our teens
And the thought of being forty was the stuff
of bad dreams?

It used to seem just SO FAR AWAY
Like the very idea of our hair going grey.

But although I saw 'forty' as a thing quite morbid
On the upside, I thought, at least by then I'll be sorted
Well that idea has been totally thwarted – I'm now well
over forty – and nowhere near sorted.

I used to imagine I'd be this elegant being
"Age forty will be so calm and so freeing."

I'd see older women who'd uplifted their faces
And wonder, Why don't they grow old with some graces?
These days – if the price was not such a huge number –
I'd scaffold my face if it made me look younger.

So, that milestone of 'forty' is finally here...
To be perfectly honest, it's been here for some years...

And I'm ashamed to tell you,
I've reached that worrying time
When 'comfort' is a clothes-buying factor of mine

(Don't get me wrong – things have not got too drastic –
my bras still offer lift and my waists aren't elastic.)

But I do find myself putting 'warmth' over 'style'
And this can lead to outfits that (my kids tell me) are vile.

Or worse, I buy clothes because I think they are 'fun'
Actually, these clothes just scream 'I'm a mum'.

I look down at my knees and they frown back at me
The skin hanging down in a semi-circular degree.

Not long ago, I hit Top Shop for 'a spree'
And realised the clothes were too young for me
(Actually, I thought, Some of this is my style,
but the salesgirl just gave me a pitying smile.)

Sometimes, I see a young girl in her prime
And bitterly think, Just you wait till your time.

And have you seen the faces of drivers these days?
Since when was twelve the legal age...?

Same thing with the youngsters I see in the pubs!
Most of them look like they could still join the Cubs!

I know... I know... it's not them, it's me
It's not possible that doctor was really age three...

And my friends these days? Where to start?
The majority of them are falling apart!
There's bad knees and backs – plus visits to quacks –
some are even failing to wax!

Although, the failing to wax is perhaps an upside
Of being the wrong side of forty-five...

I still want to look nice... I haven't given up (as such...)
But the truth of the matter is: I don't care as much.

And, to be honest, that thought is actually quite freeing
Although, I've yet to become that calm, elegant being...

Regrets... I've had a few...

Je Ne Regrette Rien

I'd love to believe in this idealistic view
That we should never regret the things that we do.

But really? Can any of us honestly say
"If I could live life again, I'd live it just the same way?"

'What doesn't kill us makes us stronger' and such
sentiments cannot be applied to past cringy events.

Personally, if I knew then what I know now
I'd never have called my first boss a 'fat cow'
(I hurt her feelings, I lost the job, I'm pretty sure in
that company I'm still known as 'that knob'.)

Then there's the things I did as a girl
The memories of which still make my toes curl.

Wetting myself on that class trip to the zoo
Is for sure an occasion I would choose NOT to do
Thus avoiding the nickname of 'soggy knickers' –
in my head, I can still hear those mean sniggers.

I would not quit piano after only a week
Or call the teacher a 'carnival freak'.

I would not beg to join Brownies on the wrong side of town
And then quit when I found out the outfit was brown
(I know... I know... I should have clocked the clue,
to the likelihood of the uniforms' hue...)

I would not quit ballet because one girl pointed and jeered
And told all the other girls my leotard was weird
I could carry on with this quitting list,
but I'm assuming by now you'll have got the gist.

Shitting myself on the school climbing frame
And letting Steve 'Shit Pants' Norton take the blame?
(Actually... this one I might still do again...)

And why oh why did I think it was cool
To wear a 'Pink Ladies' jacket to school?
Granted 'Grease' is the best film ever made,
but the sound of those jeers will never fade.

At the age of sixteen, dropping school work for boys?
Plus makeup and shopping and other such joys?
Don't get me wrong – these things have their place –
but my A Level results were, in turn, a disgrace.

I would not walk down that street in West Brom
With my skirt mortifyingly caught in my thong
This was a very long time ago –
my bum in a thong is now a NO GO.

Nor would I redo that night when I drank
An amount of tequila to fill a fish tank
It taught me no lessons – I still drink like a fish – al-
though, admittedly, I do now give tequila a miss.

Leaving details aside (in case my in-laws read this)
There's a number of men I would not have 'kissed'.

The ex that I stalked for a year and a half?
Given time again, I would not choose that path.

That time when I selfied myself in my smalls
Then accidentally pressed 'send to all'?
This memory can still make me feel sick and
bring on a case of 'sweaty upper lip'.

And as for the 'ex-boyfriend's name' tattoo
That I most certainly would not do!
(Not 'least 'cos my skin is no more in its prime,
so the lettering no longer holds a straight line.)

I would not get drunk and tell my friends
my true thoughts
Particularly, the advice 'you really should avoid shorts'.

I would not write a poem that clearly explains
It was me who shat on that climbing frame
Oh.

Small Pleasures

Much pleasure is found in the small things in life
And listed below are some joys of a wife
(At least I hope other wives see them as such,
else I fear I am sharing rather too much.)

So as a wife and a mum, and a cleaner of mess
And a cook and a driver and a—oops, I digress...

What I am really trying to say
Is that these are the things that light up my day:

When the meal you were planning on having for tea
Is in the shop with the offer 'buy two get one free'.

When the dinner guests have all buggered off home
And you can clear up the mess and drink alone.

Food that is made by somebody else
Anyone at all – just not yourself
(Well, anyone except someone else's child –
the very idea of that is just vile.)

Those vacuum cleaners that allow you to see
Just how much they've sucked up in 'carpet debris'
I know this one should make us feel sad –
it implies that the filth in our house is quite bad
But, somehow, the sight of that dusty extraction
brings me a state of great satisfaction.

Waking in the knowledge that you had sex last night
So a week (or two?) off is completely all right.

Browsing on Facebook and learning that
The cool girl from school is now rather fat
Well, at least, you can see she is fatter than you –
which, to be honest, will perfectly do.

The happy knowledge that it's Friday night
So no need for the 'school tomorrow' bedtime fight.

When your teenage daughter screams,
"You're such a witch."
And you succeed in NOT answering,
"Well, you're such a bitch."

When that same teenage child asks for a hug
You know they want something –
you're not actually a mug...
But these days, you'll take any sign of affection,
amidst the usual cloud of rejection.

The quiet satisfaction of an empty wash basket
It'll be full tomorrow – you'll blow your gasket
Much like the bin, it's either empty or bursting and the
latter state will leave you cursing.

Finding that dress you've been stalking on sale
Let's be honest – it's the freakin' Holy Grail
Admittedly, it's a little too tight when you try it... but
that's just fine as you've been meaning to diet.

Finding the shoes you've been wanting, half price!
You are certain you need them – they are just SO nice
Of course, you've nothing to match the shoes,
which means you've a whole new outfit to choose.

When your cleverer friend shame drops a book title
(it's Russian)
And for once you've read the book up for discussion
Well, 'read' is perhaps not strictly true,
but you did glance over a recent review.

Flopping down to (finally) watch TV
And finding Dirty Dancing on ITV3
It doesn't matter that you own a copy –
when it's live on TV, it makes you go soppy
(Same as a song on a radio station –
if it's one of your faves, you feel utter elation.)

When your children are actually asleep by nine
And you've poured yourself a bucket of wine.

When the wine above has hit the right place
Tiptoeing in to watch your child's sleeping face
No matter how awful their daily hysterics...
when asleep, our babies are simply angelic.

So, these are some of my happy things –
proof that we really don't need diamond rings
3need and want are different things –
I am, of course, not adverse to diamond rings...
We just need to relish the small things in life,
and if you take time to look, they truly are rife.

Don't Judge a Book by Its Cover
(or a girl by her lovers)

So we all do this thing: on the strength of one glance
We judge one another without giving a chance
As youngsters, these judgements occur far less –
not many toddlers choose friends based on dress.

But as we get older, it seems that our views
Are often biased by what we've perused.

As a race, we humans are too keen to leap
To assumptions made on things only skin deep.

It really should not be okay that we base
Our opinions on one look at a person's face
Or by their clothes – or their job or their car –
or whether or not they are wearing a bra
(Although going braless does look quite painful,
it should not cause us all to look quite so disdainful.)

Most of our towns have a local 'mad man'
Who's immediately judged to be a 'bad man'
In fact, he had the most awful childhood and is now
just greatly misunderstood.

If we see a girl in a very short skirt
We immediately brand her a bit of a flirt
In fact, this girl has low self-esteem –
there's always more to a look than what there may seem.

We wonder if that person who's a bit overweight
Really ought to eat more of that vast creamy cake

In fact, this person has clinical depression and the eating
of cake helps them through a bad session
(We all have our crutch – for me, it's the booze –
it's really not something we are able to choose.)

That celeb who we judge for being too thin
Was bullied at school for having more than one chin.

That pop star we consider should now act their age
Can only find happiness when up on that stage.

The office member we all love to hate
Would give anything to call even one of us 'mate'
(They know they're disliked and they'd love to fit in,
they just have no concept of where to begin.)

That girl on the bus? Caked in foundation?
She's covered in scars – makeup's her salvation.

That guy on the street? Who mouths 'one two three'?
He's perfectly sane – he just has OCD
He's counting his steps because his world won't feel
safe if this counting ritual is knocked out of place.

And isn't it strange that society says
That certain women are 'easy lays'?
But if a man had exactly the same sexual past
His every encounter would be proudly broadcast
"This chap is so virile, such a stud, what a MAN."
But for women: "You ought to live life like your gran!"

You hear that a girl gets 'knocked up' as a teen
And your immediate thoughts are often quite mean
What was she thinking – was she thinking at all? Did she
honestly believe his talk of 'withdrawal'?

The truth in such cases is quite often that:
She thought it was love… and he was a twat
Goodness, I think I am sounding quite sour –
can I try and label these feelings 'girl power'?

But you get my point… It should not be okay
For women to be judged in this unfair way.

There are endless examples of the judgements we cast
Shall we all try and make this a thing of the past?
Please, don't think I'm pointing fingers at you –
if you're reading this book, you'll know I judge too.

But, imagine, if looks, wealth or race weren't a 'thing'
How much more happiness this world would bring?

The Wolf in Sheep's Clothing
(The Wife in 'Cheap' Clothing)

Have you ever noticed that a woman often conceals
The cost of a dress or a new pair of heels?

For example, when someone says, "Your top's very nice"
We immediately tell them we bought it half price?

Or "Really?" We shrug (just to hide our quiet pleasure)
"This old thing? I've had it forever."

For some reason we feel the need to defend
The ways in which we have chosen to spend.

Sometimes – as above – we make up the lie
Because receiving a compliment makes us feel shy.

There is, however, a different case
When the fibs are invented just to save face.

These are the times when we know we've been bad
And the amount we have spent might make someone mad...

These fibs are often made up by a wife
And designed to fool the man in her life

(Please, don't think that I'm being sexist –
it's just a poem, don't dissect it

'Wife' or 'man' can be interchanged as you please,
with whatever label you give your own squeeze.)

So the 'wife' in this story likes to SPEND
And this habit leads her to also pretend...

Her pretences relate to the cost of her wares
Such as shoes... of which she has numerous pairs.

And dresses... whose real price she never confesses
Or how much it costs to highlight her tresses.

But it seems when the income increases in size
We also increase the "this old thing" lies.

While most of us tone down a spree in Mark One
There are others who favour Louis Vuitton
(I realise my use of 'Mark One' shows my age...
think 'Primark' if you need a more up-to-date gauge.)

With ingenuity, she has come up with many a ruse
To explain the next pair of new Jimmy Choos.

She has even excused a new diamond ring
With the age old excuse 'oh this old thing'
(You'll forgive my use of 'this old thing' thrice,
it just rolls off the tongue if shopping's your vice.)

With some of the costlier things she has bought
The wife has had to knock off a nought.

Her husband thinks she is naturally slim
He has no idea of her hours at the gym
(Nor the personal trainer or 'diet technician' –
both of whom she employs to bring 'Svelte' to fruition.)

He never questioned her fat-free limbs
And he was in the dark when she lost a few chins
(Both these procedures took place in Greece,
under the guise of a trip with her niece.)

Sometimes, the spending gets a bit out of hand
And – for a short while – the shopping is canned.

But then a message pops up in her mail
'Selfridges is having a sale!'
(Surely, to shop in a sale is okay...?
A bit like saving... in a way...?)

When the sale season rudely comes to an end
The wife feels sad... How she does like to spend!

So she cheers herself up with a browse on Zalando
"I'm sure I need knickers – I can't go commando."
(Surely, shopping online is okay...?
No need to pay for a parking bay...?)

Sometimes, the wife makes a rash declaration
"I really must stop with this shopping fixation."

She promises herself, "I will buy no more fashion."
And promptly casts round for a new shopping passion
Whether makeup or homeware, garden or skincare,
there's really no end to the ways she can spend.

But by coming up with her little pretences
The wife is happy and the man is... defenceless
To reiterate again, swap 'man' as you choose,
for the person from whom you hide *your* new shoes.

Brits Abroad

So this one's not really a proverb or saying
But we all know exactly the point I'm conveying.

A Brit abroad's the unfortunate situation
That occurs when a British family go on vacation
(Please, don't think that I am being racist –
as a Brit myself, I know our disgraces...)

This type of holiday begins with a fuss
As the family pile on to the airport bus.

By 'family', I don't just mean closest of kin
Aunties and cousins and step-siblings join in.

On airport arrival, a lost passport's discovered
There are tears – then shrieking when, at last, it's recovered
Granny had put it in her bra for safekeeping –
getting it out was what caused all the shrieking.

At check-in, the family cause a 'to do'
When Little Freddie announces he's just done a poo.

At security, the family hold up the line
When it's found Auntie Lil's tried to sneak in some wine.

In departures, Uncle Pete causes utter mayhem
With his delight at a pint in the early a.m.
(To be fair, the whole family rejoice in this pleasure –
although Boycie complains, "This gin's not a full measure.")

There's a last minute panic when boarding is called
And Pete needs to be carried from the bar where he's sprawled
Turns out five pints go straight to your head,
if drunk at an hour when you're usually in bed.

Upon boarding, the family hold up the queue
As 'Our Sharon' stops to flirt with the crew.

Once in flight, 'Big Sal' tries to hold in a poo
'Cos she thinks Ryanair charge a quid for the loo
(This incident has rather a messy result but Sal claims
to this day that it wasn't her fault.)

When they finally touch down in the exotic hot place
Most of the family are completely shit faced.

They are met by (over) enthusiastic holiday reps
And Pete takes a fall as he climbs the coach steps
The reps have seen it all before and they stoically
lift Pete off the coach floor.

Once checked in, everyone gets changed for the pool
Pete under does it – and looks like a tool
The poor other guests look on appalled –
no pair of Speedos should be quite that small

Next morning, the family head straight for the 'pub'
Where they order strong tea and 'Full English' grub
"We don't want none of this foreign muck – last year,
it left Granny awful backed up."

They quickly fall into a well-oiled routine
For the teens, it is largely based on a screen...

'Our Sharon' spends all day on a lounger
Reading magazines and pouring drinks down 'er
There's nothing like reading a sordid exposé,
while happily sipping an ice cold rosé.

'Auntie Lil' joins in with the rep run games
Which seem to be designed to cause utmost shame
"Drink this, then circle six times round a stick",
oh how we all laugh when a person is sick.

Uncle Pete is a fixture at the pool-side bar
Where he knocks back jar after jar, after jar...

Cousin Wes is the one who just never learns
And day one in the sun gives him third degree burns
This happens pretty much every time,
but he still insists Factor 2 is fine...

Little Freddie makes friends with the posh family's kid
The posh family desperately try and get rid
There's an awkward moment when the poshos are heard,
referring to Freddie as 'that little turd'.

By week two, the family need a diversion
And book themselves on to a 'cultured excursion'
They visit some ruins, sample regional liquor and
'Our Sharon' cops off with the local vicar.

There's a bit of a squabble when they do karaoke
And Pete tells 'Big Sal' that her voice is quite 'blokey'
To be honest, as the holiday comes to an end,
there are very few people Pete's failed to offend.

Check-out is early – there are headaches all round
And a last minute panic when 'Our Sharon' can't be found
Turns out she'd decided on one final shot to get
the vicar to tie the knot.

As the plane touches down, they awake from their slumbers
And the posh family try to avoid swapping numbers...

About the Author

Genevieve lives in the UK with her husband, two daughters and a very shouty sausage dog. This is her second book of poems and she very much hopes one day to have some ideas for another book. To date that isn't happening.

Acknowledgements

I would like to thank Jocelyn Palmer for
allowing me to base 'Je ne regret rien'
entirely on her life.